© 2000 by Barbour Publishing, Inc.

ISBN 1-58660-245-4

Cover art © Picture Quest

Previously released as *A Simple Christmas*.

All Scripture quotations are from the King James Version of the Bible.

Published by Barbour Books, an imprint of Barbour Publishing, Inc., P. O. Box 719, Uhrichsville, Ohio 44683 www.barbourbooks.com

 Member of the
Evangelical Christian
Publishers Association

Printed in China.
5 4 3

May the peace of Christ be yours this Christmas

Ellyn Sanna

Peace

We all know that Christmas is Jesus' birthday. But sometimes we're just so busy at Christmastime with our many responsibilities for gift giving and hospitality that the Baby's celebration gets lost in all the bustle. But despite the world's commercialism and busyness, the Christ Child is there, silent and patient; even when He is forgotten, He is still the heart that glows undimmed at the center of our shopping and baking and rushing. This year, for the Baby's sake, for our own hearts' sakes, let's take some time to simply rest beside His quiet, starlit manger.

For unto us a child is born, unto us a son is given. . .
and his name shall be called Wonderful.

ISAIAH 9:6

Contents

1

Our Hearts' Desires at Christmas

The aspects of things that are most important for us
are hidden because of their simplicity and familiarity.

LUDWIG WITTGENSTEIN

PEACEFUL HEART, PEACEFUL CHRISTMAS

I'm going to do it differently this year, I used to tell myself every December 1. This year I'm going to take time for the spiritual meaning of Christmas. This year—somehow—I'll fit in more time for God. But every year, the days would rush by, a blur of shopping and cooking and family gatherings, until, finally, January 2 would dawn. Exhausted and overfed, I'd head back to work, relieved that the holidays were over at last for anot' year. And inside my heart, a disappointed child's voice would cry, *missed Christmas again. It's over—and I never recaptured the magic of childhood, the wonder of Bethlehem. I never made time for the Baby Jesus.*

This year would probably have been like all the others. I would have written Jesus on my to-do list, but as the days sped past, somehow that one Christmas "responsibility" would never get accomplished. Like always, I was overcommitted, and on the first Sunday of December, I was on my way to speak to a church group on "Simplifying Christmas: Juggling Our Lives during Advent." The topic was pretty ironic: I was juggling my own life so furiously that I really didn't have time for this talk.

As I made the forty-five-minute drive to the church where I'd be speaking, I was longing for a quiet evening at home. I had made the commitment, though, and obviously, I couldn't back out now. So as I drove, I reviewed the topics I would cover in my talk, points that would touch on goal-setting and time management. I had a hard time focusing. Here I was at the very beginning of Advent, and already I was so tired I could barely

concentrate. I felt overwhelmed.

Sometimes, though, God speaks to us most clearly when we're at our weakest. That night, in the midst of my exhaustion, I began to wonder what my own goals for Advent really were. At first the ideas popped into my head automatically: Spend more time with my family; do things more simply this year; get my shopping done early. . . . They were all good goals, but something pulled my thoughts deeper. *What is your heart's desire?* a quiet voice seemed to ask me.

So that night, I didn't talk about goals after all; instead, I spoke about our deepest hearts' desires. And as we talked and prayed together, I knew what my own heart was crying out for: I wanted Jesus. I had made my life so complicated when really it was very simple; Christ alone was the answer to my heart's yearning and emptiness. All the other Christmas trappings were just extras I could do without.

This past Advent, I never did get all my Christmas cards written—and I didn't bake even one batch of cookies. But I knew what my heart's desire was—and He was right there with me as I shopped in the mall, as I wrapped gifts, as I left things undone and simply sat quietly in His presence early in the morning.

If we pare away the nonessentials, we're left with what really matters. Christ's coming does not depend on our efforts, and simpler lives have more room in them for God. Most of all, when we simplify our hearts, then, at last, a peaceful Christmas will finally be ours.

CHRISTMAS CELEBRATIONS

Over the centuries, Christmas traditions have radically changed. The Christmas celebration itself once lasted for days without much advance planning; now the reverse is true: We spend an entire month preparing for one day. Many folk and religious traditions—such as dancing, music-making, and game-playing—have been replaced by what seems to be America's biggest Christmas tradition: shopping. We measure Advent in terms of "shopping days," and we culminate these frantic weeks with a gift-opening ritual that is often almost as frantic. And then Christmas comes to an abrupt end.

Christmas should be a family time, but, oddly enough, surveys show that we spend less time with our immediate families during the month of December than at any other time. What is more, researchers tell us there is a 15 percent increase in the number of people seeking help for depression at this time of year. We work so hard to make our Christmases magic and meaningful; no wonder we get depressed when we're left with hearts that are empty and lonely.

In reality, shared experiences, not objects or gifts, are the things that remain in our hearts the longest. As families, we need to determine what we truly long for at Christmas—and then we must choose to celebrate the traditions that will help us to capture the essence of those longings.

A word of warning, though: Sometimes our traditions, if held too tightly, can rob us of our Christmas joy. Be sure your traditions point you to Jesus.

A CELEBRATION
OF THE HEART

On December 1, after months of danger and fear, Lupe left her home in Central America and arrived in the United States. She and her mother and her four children settled into an apartment in New York City, and Lupe set to work turning her family into Americans.

There were countless offices to visit, papers to fill out, and bus schedules to learn, but Lupe was so excited at being in America at last that she never complained. While her children were at school, she dashed around the city. She was proud of herself, too, that she hadn't forgotten Christmas; she had bags of Christmas gifts, an artificial tree, and packages of tinsel and red balls stashed in her bedroom closet. This year her family would have a truly American Christmas. Their new neighbors were coming to dinner on December 20, and they would see just how well Lupe and her family fit in.

She never asked her mother what she was doing every day while Lupe took care of business. But on December 20, when Lupe rushed home just in time to decorate the apartment and prepare the meal, she found a surprise waiting.

All the while Lupe was out of the apartment, her mother's arthritic hands had slowly and painstakingly cut out shapes of birds and stars from bright bits of felt. She had embroidered them with crimson thread, and now they hung on a crooked, half-dead evergreen tree she had found discarded in the alley.

No, thought Lupe, *I can't let the neighbors see this tree.* She took a slow step closer, not ready to meet her mother's eyes. And then she noticed that instead of a star or an angel, at the top of the tree was a scarlet heart. The names of Lupe, her mother, and each of the children were embroidered on the heart in gold. Lupe turned toward her mother, wondering what this tree topper meant.

Her mother smiled. "Last year at Christmas, we were so afraid," she said softly. "But this year, we have nothing to fear. I wanted to thank the Christ Child." Her faded eyes were bright with joy. "He has granted me the desires of my heart. That is what I celebrate this year at Christmas."

Lupe looked at the crooked tree. She straightened her shoulders and let out a long breath. This, she realized, was the very best tree her family could have.

For me, the spirit of Christmas is about letting the loving
but messy little rituals become just as important as the solemn
and graceful ones. It's about making room for everyone.
ANN MICHAEL

. . .

Thou hast given him
his heart's desire, and hast not
withholden the request of his lips.

PSALM 21:2

. . .

There's room in my heart, Lord Jesus,
There's room in my heart for You.
GOSPEL CHORUS

2

Freeing Christmas from the Trap of Consumerism

For where your treasure is,
there will your heart be also.

LUKE 12:34

 *May the Peace of Christ*

THE OTHER SHEPHERD

Asa watched the other shepherds hurry off toward Bethlehem. He shook his head. This wasn't like them. Jacob, Benjamin, and Nathanael were usually practical men, not given to whims or flights of fancy. They knew watching the sheep was serious work that could not be shirked on an impulse. If the four of them ever hoped to make any money off these animals, then the flock had to be tended carefully and consistently, each moment of the day and night. Shepherds couldn't just go traipsing off to Bethlehem in the middle of the night.

The first half of the night had been Benjamin's turn to keep watch, and Asa had fallen into exhausted sleep almost as soon as his head touched the bunched-up cloak he used for a pillow. When he awoke, the others were on their feet, staring up at the sky. Asa had a feeling that a clap of thunder and lightning might have woken him; at any rate, a strange golden glow was fading from the starlit heavens.

The other three men were so shaken they could barely speak. They babbled about angels and a baby—and almost immediately, they had begun running away from the sheep and over the hills toward town.

Asa shook his head again, then turned back to the flock. Carefully, he counted each one. In his head, he added up the profit he could expect from their wool. Let the others go chasing dreams. At least he for one had his priorities straight. He settled himself on the cold, dark hillside. As he once again tallied his investment in the sheep, he never dreamed what he had missed.

If you get simple beauty and nought else;
You get about the best thing God invents.
ROBERT BROWNING

. . .

*It is in the enjoyment
and not in mere possession that
makes for happiness.*

MICHEL DE MONTAIGNE

. . .

You were made for enjoyment,
and the world was filled with things which you will enjoy,
unless you are too proud to be pleased with them,
or too grasping to care for what you cannot turn
to other account than mere delight.
JOHN RUSKIN

FREE TO BELIEVE
THE TRUTH

God gave us the material world to enjoy. At Christmastime, I think He expects us to delight our hearts in the scents and sights and sounds of the holidays. But material things in and of themselves do not bring happiness, emotional fulfillment, or a sense of connection to others or to God.

Unfortunately, we Americans have become so focused on the material world—things that can be bought and paid for—that every year we spend more at Christmas than we can afford. Holiday displays in stores across our land are designed to inspire us to buy, buy, buy—and as a result, debt counselors are busiest in January and February as people struggle to catch up after their shopping sprees. But Christmas is not something that can be purchased. At the true center of Christmas's heart is the grace of God—and grace has nothing to do with money.

That doesn't mean we can't enjoy the decorations that fill the streets and malls or the holiday excitement that hums through all the stores throughout December. It's easy to point disapproving fingers at our culture's neurotic consumerism, blaming society for the sickness in our own hearts. But the first step to changing the world around us is to change what's inside us. True freedom comes from within.

If we allow even the most commercial decorations to point our hearts toward the Christ Child, toward the love He wants us to share with others, then we can joyfully appreciate them. After all, we know the real secret of Christmas. We don't have to buy the lie the world wants us to believe.

Christmas is the most human and kindly of seasons,
as fully penetrated and irradiated with the feeling of
human brotherhood, which is the essential spirit of Christianity,
as the month of June with sunshine and the balmy breath of roses.
GEORGE WILLIAM CURTIS

• • •

He is a wise man who
does not grieve for the
things which he has not,
but rejoices for those which he has.
EPICTETUS

• • •

Heap on more wood—the wind is chill;
But let it whistle as it will,
We'll keep our Christmas merry still.
SIR WALTER SCOTT

POVERTY

All poor men and humble,
All lame men who stumble,
Come haste ye, nor feel ye afraid;
For Jesus, our treasure,
With love past all measure,
In lowly poor manger was laid.

Though wise men who found Him
Laid rich gifts around Him,
Yet oxen they gave Him their hay:
And Jesus in beauty
Accepted their duty;
Contented in manger He lay.

OLD WELSH CAROL,
translated by K. E. ROBERTS

3

Like Little Children

Whosoever shall not receive the kingdom of God
as a little child shall in no wise enter therein.

LUKE 18:17

A CHILD'S PERCEPTION

"You know what the Baby Jesus is?" my six year old asked me this Christmas.

"What?" I asked absently, struggling to get our Christmas tree lights evenly distributed.

"The Baby Jesus," she announced, "is what God's love looked like when He turned it into a person."

I don't know if theologians would agree with all the ramifications of her statement. But I do know that my children often seem to have an instinctive insight into spiritual things that wakes up my grown-up understanding.

At Christmastime, children play an essential part in our celebrations. So much of what we do is intended to please them—and all the while our hearts keep hearkening back to the Christmas memories of our own childhoods. On Christmas Eve, sometimes we can't help but envy our children the stars in their eyes, especially when our own eyes are dull with exhaustion.

Christmas is so much simpler for a child. Can we open our tired adult hearts to that same simplicity?

*Happy, happy Christmas,
that can win us back to the
delusions of our childish days,
recall to the old man
the pleasures of his youth. . . .*

CHARLES DICKENS

Children aren't perfect, of course. They can be selfish, acquisitive little creatures, all too eager to point out to their parents the multitude of gifts they want for Christmas. As adults, however, we can choose to acknowledge that children really need and want five basic things for Christmas:

- relaxed and loving times with the family
- realistic expectations about gifts
- an evenly paced holiday season that allows for normal amounts of sleep
- strong family traditions
- a sense of the season's spiritual meaning

MAKE TIME
FOR CHILDHOOD

Because of holiday pressures, children are apt to receive less attention from their parents during December than at any other time of the year—only to be heaped with gifts on Christmas day. If we are to honor the Child Whose birth we celebrate, and if we are to have a child's simplicity within our own hearts, then we must set firm priorities for our families, making sure our children are included in holiday activities at home—such as baking cookies and decorating the tree (even if it means less beautiful cookies and Christmas trees). Being together, demonstrating our love to one another in simple, childlike ways, celebrates Christ's birth far better than the most beautiful and magazine-perfect holiday craft or baked good.

Surely I have behaved and quieted myself, as a child. . . .

PSALM 131:2

In the depth of winter,
when nature lies wrapped in her shroud of sheeted snow. . .
heart calls unto heart;
and we draw our pleasures from the deep wells of loving kindness
which lie in the quiet recesses of our bosoms,
and which, when resorted to,
furnish forth the pure element of domestic felicity.
WASHINGTON IRVING, *Old Christmas*

• • •

The people who find the most pleasure in Christmas are
the ones who have taken control of the celebration and
shaped it to conform to their own wishes and values.
They know what's most important about Christmas to them,
and they've found ways to make those values come alive.
JO ROBINSON

A CHILD'S JOY

"Why are you bothering with that?"

Jane glanced up at her husband. "Because the children will love it." Her voice was edged with irritation. She took a deep breath, and for the second time spread a thin line of frosting along the slab of cake that was meant to be the back wall of the gingerbread house she was building. For the second time, all four walls collapsed as soon as she set the last wall in place.

"Why don't you let the children help you? Might be more fun that way."

"For heaven's sake, Dan," Jane snapped, struggling to control her frustration. "If I can't get it right, can you imagine what a mess they'd make?"

Dan shrugged into his winter jacket. "Does it really matter if it's not perfect?" he asked mildly.

Jane didn't even bother to answer.

When the fourth wall was at last in place, she looked up. Through the kitchen window, she could see Dan and the kids sliding on cookie sheets down the slope behind the house. She sighed. So that was where her cookie sheets had gone. How did they expect her to bake eight dozen Christmas cookies without cookie sheets?

How nice it must be to be a man or a child at Christmastime, she thought to herself. *Men and children aren't responsible for all the baking and cleaning and decorating; they can simply enjoy themselves.* Fuming, she turned her attention to the gingerbread house's roof. Carefully, gently, she set it in place. *Oh, thank goodness; everything looks just the way it does in the picture.* Now all she had to do was decorate it.

As she rummaged in the cupboard for food coloring to add to the frosting, her youngest child stuck his head in the back door. "Come out and play with us, Mommy."

Jane added a few drops of red to the frosting and began to stir. "You can see I'm busy, Will."

"Well, when won't you be busy?"

Jane sighed for the second time in five minutes. "After Christmas is over."

Will's forehead puckered. He stood in the door watching her as she began to edge the gingerbread roof with pink.

"Go on now," Jane said absently. "You're letting in the cold."

Will heaved a sigh of his own and disappeared, slamming the door behind him. Immediately, with a slow inevitability that reminded Jane of the sinking of the *Titanic,* the gingerbread house began to sag until, despite her frantic efforts, it collapsed into a heap of brown crumbs and pink frosting.

The jar of the door going shut must have been what did it. Or maybe it would have happened anyway. Maybe the cake was too warm, or maybe she had put in too much milk. . . . Jane sank down on the kitchen floor and cried.

Her family found her there. They gathered around her, frightened by her tears. They smothered her with hugs and showered her with kisses. Then her oldest took a bite of the ruined gingerbread house and tried to comfort her by saying, "It tastes good anyway."

"Does it?" Jane gulped. "Let's see."

Her daughter handed her a bite. It did taste good.

Dan picked up the plate. "Go on." He grinned at her. "Have another piece."

Jane took the plate from him and hesitated. Then she set the gingerbread house on the floor in front of her. "Oh, well," she quavered. "We might as well enjoy it."

Her children looked at her to see if she meant it. And then the whole family settled on the floor around the plate, stuffing their faces with the crumbs.

"This is way more fun than any regular gingerbread house," her middle child said.

Will looked up at her, frosting smeared across his cheeks, his eyes bright with joy. "Does this mean you can come sledding with us now?"

4

Practical Strategies for a Peaceful Christmas

What is your heart's desire for Advent? Whatever it is, does it depend on you doing each and every thing on your to-do list? This year, evaluate your list realistically. Highlight the things you truly love doing. Circle the ones that exhaust you the most. If some of your highlighted items are also circled, then they're probably worth your effort. But are all of the items you circled really necessary? What would happen if you simply didn't do them? Would Christmas grind to a halt this year?

May the Peace of Christ

Here is another practical strategy to determine how much you should take on at Christmas:

1. Make a thorough checklist of your obligations for the month of December, including:
   - work responsibilities
   - activities involving your children
   - church commitments or other volunteer activities
   - family gatherings
2. Decide how many hours of free time a day you generally have.
3. How do you usually spend this free time?
4. When preparing for Christmas, what do you usually take time from?

Answering these questions will help you see the cost of your holiday preparations in terms of time and energy. Are all of your commitments truly worth their cost? Or can you find your heart's desire this Christmas even if you leave some of these things undone?

MOTIVATED BY LOVE

When we work so hard at our preparations for Christmas, we often feel cheated and frustrated when others fail to notice the results of all our efforts. We need to ask ourselves why we are doing the things we choose to do. If love motivates us—love for our families, for our neighbors, for Jesus—then we are free to simply enjoy the actual process of what we do, rather than requiring the approval and admiration of others for the results of our labors.

Christmas is about the birth of Love into our world—and we celebrate this by spending time with the people God has given us. Some practical ways to spend more time at Christmas with the people we love are:

- Take extra time off from work.
- Simplify holiday preparations.
- Entertain less.
- Attend fewer parties that are just for adults.
- Be more relaxed about how the house looks.
- Cut back on outside commitments.
- Make fewer gifts.
- Watch less television.
- Travel less.

Some activities to bring your family together and add some fun to the holidays:

- winter sports (skating, sledding, hockey)
- game-playing
- playing musical instruments
- reading aloud to each other
- attending concerts
- telling family stories
- cooking together
- going for walks
- creating skits and plays
- caroling

Basic ideas to keep in mind for a peaceful Christmas:

- Being together is what counts, not the perfection of your sur-
  roundings. (Jesus' coming does not depend on tasteful decorations, the cleanliness of your home, or sumptuous baked goods.)
- Everyone's comfort level and ability to relax are the keys to
  happy times together. Don't pack in too many organized activities.
- Spending the holidays with a smaller group of people with whom
  you are really close is more pleasant and less stressful than shar-
  ing it with a larger, noisier crowd of people you may not know
  as well.
- Don't feel pressured to prepare full, sit-down feasts. Encourage
  others to bring a dish to pass—or make some holiday gatherings a
  time to chat over desserts.
- Don't allow your elaborate plans for Christmas to get in the way
  of your enjoyment of what actually happens. No plan is foolproof,
  and mistakes and delays take all of us by surprise. Remember
  that the love you share while you're together is the most
  important thing.

- Holiday craft and baking ideas can add to the enjoyment of the Christmas celebration, but they are not essential to a good family Christmas. They can, in fact, take vital energy away from more important matters. We could all make do with simpler gifts and less sugar at Christmastime, but if you believe something is truly essential to your celebration, then store-bought items are often just as good. Or purchase crafts and baked goods from a church bazaar or craft sale. That way you will be benefiting a good cause, as well.

- The world will not end if you do not send a Christmas card to each and every person you know. Try shortening your list by sending cards only to those people you do not see regularly. Or send cards to half of your list (or even one-third) now, and the other half (or second third) on Valentine's Day (and, perhaps, the final third at Easter).

May the Peace of Christ

Christmas is not only a time to share our love with our families; it is also a time to spread Christ's love throughout the world around us. Here are some simple, thoughtful things to do at Christmas:

- Take home-baked goodies to older people in the neighborhood who can't get home to their families for Christmas.
- Given the typically colder weather at Christmastime, go through your winter clothing to find things you can no longer use and donate to people who need them.
- Knowing how many times families at Christmas experience a real hardship trying to give their children the holiday they'd like, why not surprise someone by anonymously paying off their layaway bill at a department store?
- To encourage children to realize the satisfaction that comes from generosity at this time of year, set an example for them through your own charitable acts and donations.

- If your family is comfortable with the Santa Claus myth, tell your children that not only does Santa Claus bring gifts, he is also happy to take any old toys or possessions left under the tree for him to recycle for some other needy child.
- If you are the parent of adult children, rather than insisting that the extended family get together every year on Christmas day, why not agree to get together on an alternate date (for instance, Epiphany Sunday after Christmas or the third Saturday of December each year)? This allows the smaller nuclear families to spend Christmas day together—and on December 25, you can volunteer to help out at a homeless shelter, hospice center, or Ronald McDonald house.
- Use some of the money you normally spend on family gifts and entertaining for a donation to a charity organization that helps children and communities in third-world countries.

Some strategies for cutting back on gift-giving expenses:

- To prevent overspending and last-minute shopping, shop throughout the year, taking advantage of sales.
- Request that relatives (such as grandparents) give only one Christmas gift per child—but suggest that instead, they spend a special day with each child on some kind of outing (watching a play, a trip to a museum, etc.) during the month of December. This also allows the parents some time to work on Christmas preparations, while giving the children quality time with grandparents.
- Or ask that extended family members give gifts for the entire family, such as games and books, and leave the individual presents for birthdays. This helps put the focus on the family as a whole.

If you would like to escape the world's focus on commercialism and draw more attention to the fact that Christmas is a celebration of Christ's birthday, here are some ideas:

- Hang stockings for everyone in the family with an extra one for Baby Jesus. Children can fill the stocking with small toys of their own they are willing to share with those children who, like the Baby Jesus, have very little.
- Ask your children to write birthday cards to Jesus expressing their love.
- Have a birthday party, complete with a cake, for Jesus.
- Decorate with the nativity scene about a week before Christmas, leaving the appearance of the Baby Jesus for Christmas morning, with the wise men showing up on Epiphany. This helps make the story more real for children (and reminds us grown-ups, too).
- Allow your children to dress up in robes and towels to reenact Jesus' birth.
- Make it a family tradition to read the Christmas story from Luke every Christmas Eve.

Here are some Christmas classics your family might also enjoy reading aloud together:

A Child's Christmas in Wales by Dylan Thomas
Old Christmas by Washington Irving
"The Gift of the Magi" by O. Henry
A Christmas Memory by Truman Capote
On the Banks of Plum Creek by Laura Ingalls Wilder
Little Women by Louisa May Alcott
"The Fir Tree" by Hans Christian Andersen
Amahl and the Night Visitors by Gian-Carlo Menotti
"A Visit from St. Nicholas" by Clement Moore
A Christmas Carol by Charles Dickens

5

The One
Essential Thing

Thou art careful and troubled about many things:
But one thing is needful. . . .

LUKE 10:41–42

At Christmastime, it's easy to be like Martha, anxious and troubled by our many responsibilities. We're so tired, so overwhelmed; we have so much to do. We don't live in Charles Dickens's nineteenth-century society where Christmas was a time of games, song, and dance; our culture has lost many of its traditions, and instead, commercialism has become the common denominator that provides structure and meaning to our holiday.

But we don't have to let our culture rule our hearts. And we don't have to be Marthas. Instead, we can be like Mary, who relaxed in the Lord's presence. We can choose to have a peaceful and holy Christmas—because ultimately, only one thing is essential to our Christmas celebration: Jesus Christ.

• • •

Then let us all rejoice
On Christmas day, on Christmas day;
Then let us all rejoice
On Christmas day in the morning.
OLD ENGLISH CAROL